WALK AMBLESIDE, RYDAL
and GRASMERE

TWENTY WALKS AROUND
AMBLESIDE, WATERHEAD, RYDAL, AND
GRASMERE

*Bill
Birkett*

BY BILL BIRKETT

BB

BILL BIRKETT PUBLISHING

PUBLISHED BY BILL BIRKETT PUBLISHING

This book is dedicated to all who love these wonderful places.

Cover photograph: Over Grasmere Lake towards the village.
Backcover photograph: Red squirrels in Easedale.
Page [i] photograph: Above Grasmere, through the meadows on the Easedale Road.

All photographs from the Bill Birkett Photo Library
Maps by Martin Bagness based on pre-1950 Ordnance Survey maps. Completely redrawn 2010.

First published in the UK in 2010
Copyright © Bill Birkett 2010

Bill Birkett has asserted his right to be identified as author of this work in accordance wth the Copyright, Designs and Patents Act, 1988.

All rights reserved. No part of this publication may be reproduced, stored in a retrieval system, or transmitted, in any form or by any means, electronic or mechanical, by photocopying, recording or otherwise, without prior permission in writing from the publisher.

A catalogue record for this book is available from The British Library

ISBN 978-0-9564296-1-2

Book Design by Bill Birkett
Advertising Design, Management and Editing Sue Birkett
Printed in Bowness by Badger Press
for Bill Birkett Publishing
www.billbirkett.co.uk
Little Langdale, Cumbria, LA22 9NY

DISCLAIMER
Walking in the country and over the fells is potentially dangerous activity and each individual following the routes described within this book is responsible for their own safety and actions. Neither the author nor the publisher accepts any reponsibility for the individual safety or actions of anyone using this book. Although the author encountered no difficulty of access on the routes described, and while considerable effort has been made to avoid so doing, the inclusion of a route does not imply that a right of way or right of access exists in every case or in all circumstances. Readers are also advised that changes can occur to the landscape that may affect the contents of this book. The author welcomes notification of any such changes.

Tel:
015394 37272

email:
olddungeonghyll1@btconnect.com

www.odg.co.uk

A Real Escape
No TV. No Radio. No Newspapers. One of the last places in the Lake District where you can relax with real peace and tranquillity

The Old Dungeon Ghyll Hotel

A unique hotel situated in the remote and unspoilt Langdale Valley

Our Hotel and Famous Climbers/Hikers Bar offer Homemade food and a selection of real ales

Lunch time Bar Meals served from 12 noon to 2pm
Evening Bar Meals served from 6pm to 9pm

Wi-fi is available if essential ❀ We are Child & Dog Friendly

The hotel is accessible on public transport via a bus from Ambleside

CONTENTS

AMBLESIDE, RYDAL AND GRASMERE

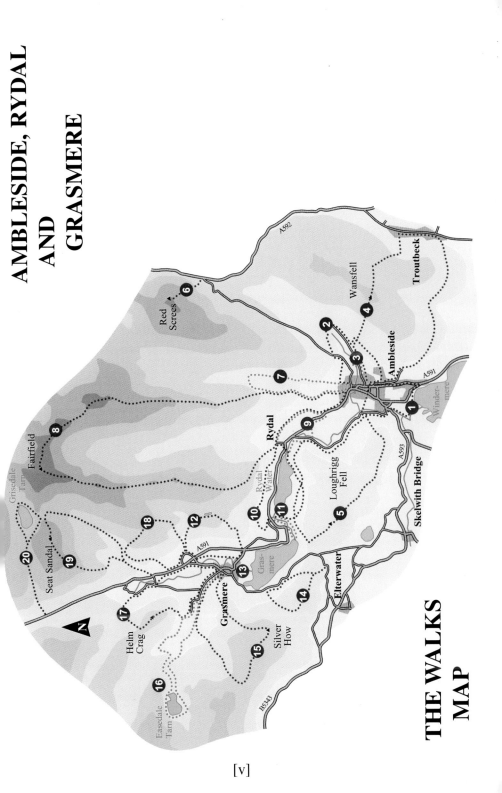

THE WALKS MAP

[v]

WALK AMBLESIDE, RYDAL AND GRASMERE
INTRODUCTION

Running as one continuous valley, set deep amongst the fells, the wooded and lake filled vales of Grasmere, Rydal and Ambleside, twist south and eastwards from Dunmail Pass in the north to Lake Windermere's Waterhead in the south. They travel an area of intense, breathtaking, beauty and are known and celebrated worldwide for their association with William Wordsworth and the Lake's Poets. Reflected through the varying moods of lake, wood and high fell, every season is markedly different. Add to this the quiet network of pathways leading by wood and water, the freedom of access over both high and low fell, and you have one of the finest and best loved walking arenas in Britain.

Founded on a lifetime's local knowledge this is a practical walking guidebook. It offers a mixture of routes of varying length and difficulty; the high and low level fells, the rivers, waterfalls, woods, through the quarries and by the ancient byways and paths passing by farm, cottage and over stone arch bridge. The walks are all circular and whatever the season or prevailing weather (within reason of course – be sensible) there is a good spread of choice here for most people. Furthermore, there are many excellent inns, cafes and places of rest, on or nearby all of these walks. These are detailed in the Fact Sheet.

The format of this inexpensive guide is simple and straightforward. The **overall maps**, on the back cover and within the contents page (page v), show immediately where the individual walks lie. Each **numbered walk** is described on a double page spread, you don't need to turn the page mid walk, with a suitably **detailed map** that can form the basis of the walk (although it is recommended that you also take an OS map with you for detailed reference and navigation, particularly on the high fells). My **photographs** illustrate some of the highlights and capture the general ambiance of the walk. The **Fact Sheet** provides the essential information and identifies places to eat, drink, rest, shelter on each individual walk. The **ringbinding** keeps the guidebook flat in your pocket and always allows it to remain open on the page of your chosen walk. Selected **adverts** provide information on local facilities that I can personally recommend.

It is quite astonishing that within this area you can enjoy one of the best loved high mountain outings in Britain - the classic Fairfield Horseshoe (Walk 8), explore the regions most interesting and popular low level fell – the many facets of intriguing Loughrigg (Walk 5), and follow the acclaimed low level 'Round of Rydal Water' (Walk 10), considered to be one of the best ten walks in Europe; only three of the twenty markedly contrasting routes that I have selected in this guide.

At the heads and feet of the vales are the settlements of Grasmere village, the hamlet of Rydal and the little town of Ambleside. Each of these settlements, within the body of the individual vales, are accompanied by their own stretch of water; Grasmere and Rydal with their little lakes and Ambleside's Waterhead with Windermere, the largest lake of all. In proportion to and blending with their natural surroundings, they all have much intrinsic and historical interest. Additionally, along with the nearby Langdales, they offer a huge choice of high quality catering and accommodation, a range of fine hotels, quaint village inns, bed and breakfast establishments, self catering cottages, cafés and bars. Whether you want to put your feet up enroute, enjoy a pint, cup of tea or a bar meal, or savour an evening meal of gourmet quality, it's available locally.

In Grasmere's Dove Cottage, see Walk 12, Willliam Wordsworth composed some of his best known poetry. However he lived at Rydal Mount, see Walks 9 and 10, from 1813 until his death in 1850. Inspired by this landscape Wordsworth and 'The Lake Poets' broke with the conventions of the day to explore the worlds of nature and human emotion in a new poetic language. Wordsworth became Poet Laureate and his 'Intimations of Immortality' is generally considered to be one of the finest poems ever written in the English language.

"Thanks to the human heart by which we live,
Thanks to its tenderness, its joys, and fears
To me the meanest flower that blows can give
Thoughts that do often lie too deep for tears."

It was while living at Rydal that his most famous poem 'Daffodils' was published in 1815. Although the poem may be classed a 'lightweight' compared to his other works it remains incredibly popular. To this day, some two hundred years after it was written, most people can quote a part, if not all, of the poem. Interestingly, if local folklore is to be believed, William's sister Dorothy played much more than a peripheral role in all these works.

Following the success of "Walk The Langdales" this is the second illustrated guidebook in the series published by **Bill Birkett Publishing.** The books are available both locally and nationally through various outlets and bookshops and signed copies are available directly from my website **www.billbirkett.co.uk**

CAUTION

Particularly on the fells it is important that walkers have equipment appropriate to both prevailing and possible conditions. Suitable footwear, weatherproof clothing, map and compass or GPS, are essential requirements. Watch to each step. For guidance on navigation, clothing and footwear in both summer and winter, survival and tips on digital photography, see "The Hillwalker's Manual" by Bill Birkett.

WALK 1
WATERHEAD TO AMBLESIDE VIA TWO PARKS, TWO RIVERS AND THE ROMAN FORT
(PLUS ALTERNATIVE – A CLIMB TO TODD CRAGS)

A pleasant walk from Waterhead to Ambleside. It takes a route through Borran's Park, by Galava Roman Fort, on beside the Serpentine to pass the confluence of the Rivers Rothay and Brathay before crossing the Rothay footbridge. A level walk continues along the Under Loughrigg Road to gain the entrance to Rothay Park. Alternatively follow the road to Clappersgate to ascend Todd Crags - a wonderful viewpoint. Rothay Park leads to the spired St Mary's Church and return to Waterhead along Lake Road.

THE ROUTE
Gain the lakeside and continue along the path to pass the Wateredge Inn. Turn left to enter Borrans Park. Pass the shelter and continue by the water's edge until the path bears away to the right. A little iron kissing gate on the left enters the field containing Galava Roman Fort.

On the far left, beyond the fenced areas, a little gate leads off to a riverside path. To the left lies The Serpentine, once a favourite local swimming area.

◆ Continue by the riverside, passing the confluence of the rivers Brathay and Rothay, until a footbridge leads left over the Rothay. For the regular low

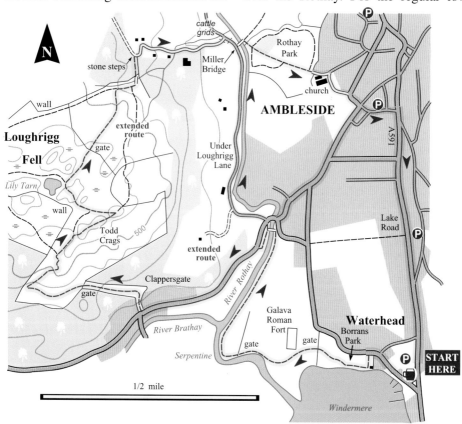

WALK 1

From Todd Crag over Waterhead

path descends to the right from the tarn. At the base of the slope a little footbridge leads to the left. Follow a short path between the trees until stone steps drop to a track. Descend steeply to the Under Loughrigg Road and turn right to cross the cattle

level route, go right and cross the busy road to gain the quiet Under Loughrigg Road which runs besides the tree lined Rothay. In 800m the stone arched Miller Bridge leads off right into Rothay Park.
◆ For the alternative, turn left after the footbridge. Follow the footpath to the hamlet of Clappersgate. To the right, before the road junction, a narrow tree clad stony lane climbs up through the buildings. Follow the lane until it leaves the woods by a gate. A path leads off left contouring around the rock knoll, note the Sid Cross Memorial Bench, before ascending the hillside. By the edge of Fishgarths Wood the path zigs to the right then climbs to pass a boggy hollow. The rocky knolls to the right are collectively known as Todd Crags and, with a little scrambly ascent, offer open views over Waterhead and down Lake Windermere, over Ambleside to Wansfell and over Rydal to the Fairfield Horseshoe.
◆ Descend to the main path and follow it left to Lily Tarn. A well defined

grid. Immediately left is Miller Bridge.
◆ Cross the bridge and go right to take the surfaced footway through the park. Exit by iron gates with St Mary's Church to the right. Walk on then go right through the church gates and follow the lane round and out left to emerge onto the end of Compston Road. Pass White Platts Recreation Ground and go straight across the (busy) road at the junction. Keep on to pass the library and up to Lake Road. Turn right and follow the pavement until steps descend to Waterhead car park.

FACT SHEET
LENGTH: *4km (6¾km with alt).*
TIME: *1½ hours (2½ hours with alt).*
DIFFICULTY: *Easy (Mildly difficult + 200m ascent on Alternative).*
START & FINISH: *Waterhead car park (376033) or Steamer/Boat Piers.*
ALTERNATIVE START: *Ambleside; Kelsick and Lake Road car parks.*
MAPS: *OS L90 or OL7.*
HOSTELRIES: *Extensive choice at Waterhead and Ambleside.*

WALK 2
BY BLUE HILL AND ROUNDHILL FARM

Though Blue Hill gasworks have long gone and Kelsick Grammar School stands empty, Roundhill is still a working farm. Easy stony lanes, incredible trees, wonderful views to the south and west over Ambleside and the old Kelsick Grammar School and north to Kirkstone Pass, combine with a tour of Ambleside and a glimpse of a stone built farm, to make this one of the most pleasant and enjoyable walks in the region.

THE ROUTE

Opposite the car park, rise with Old Lake Road until at the top of the hill bear left rising by the Blue Hill Road. Keep on through the houses until the going levels. Keep straight on until the road becomes a stone track and quits the town.

◆ Follow the track rising above Ambleside and Kelsick Grammar School, open and expansive view to the left, to traverse the hillside until just beyond a final stand of ancient ash there is a kissing gate through the stone wall which bars the track. Go left and drop down the field, by the beck, to gain the surfaced lane. Turn right and follow the road until, on passing the house of Low Grove, down to the left, and a cattle grid, a flattish and muddy track leads off down to the left.

◆ Descend to the beck of Stock Ghyll and cross by a footbridge. Go left until a track winds up right to enter the lane beneath Roundhill Farm. Bear left along the lane until it joins the Kirkstone Road. Turning left, descend until in 200m a gated stony track, signed Public Footpath Ellerigg, leads off to the right. Follow the lane, views between the trees over Ambleside, until a stile leads to a field by a little stone shed. Go left keeping low to stone squeeze stile through the wall. Keep left making slight descent, following the path above the trees, to the bottom corner of the field.

◆ Stone slabs cross the little Eller beck to a tiny iron gated squeeze stile over the wall. Keep down the narrow lane until it becomes surfaced. Continue straight across the junction, following the high lane which leads to the surfaced

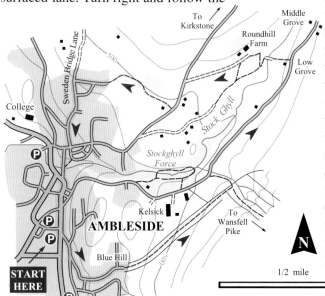

WALK 2

Over the old Kelsick Grammar School which once offered locals a world class education

Hen at Roundhill Farm

FACT SHEET
LENGTH: 5¼ km.
TIME: 1¾ hours.
DIFFICULTY: *Easy with moderate ascent (225m) and descent.*
START & FINISH: *Lake Road car park (376042).*
ALTERNATIVE START: *Any of the Ambleside car parks.*
MAPS: *OS L90 or OL7.*
HOSTELRIES: *Extensive choice in Ambleside. The farm sells eggs.*

Sweden Bridge Lane. Go left dropping to the main Kirkstone Road. Descend then bear left, above The Golden Rule Inn, to follow down North Road to the Market Cross marking the centre of Ambleside. Left, following the main road, returns to the car park.

Ancient ash beside the track

WALK 3
AMBLESIDE'S BRIDGE HOUSE TO STOCKGHYLL WATERFALLS

In past times the tumbling beck of Stockghyll turned numerous waterwheels to power the industries of Ambleside. This route walks by the ghyll, initially passing two waterwheels and the Bridge House before following Stockghyll Lane to enter oak woods. An anticlockwise circuit around the highest waterfall - Stockghyll Force – crosses the beck by two footbridges before returning to the lane.

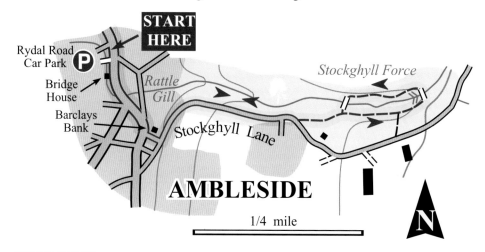

THE ROUTE

Especially after, or during, rain the tree lined waterfalls of Stockghyll are spectacular and invigorating and the woods delightful at any time of the year. There are paths throughout this walk, though the going in places can be a little rough and muddy. Cross the footbridge from the car park and turn right to pass the GlassHouse waterwheel followed by the curious Bridge House. Across the road a way through the buildings opens to the left – Rattle Gill. Beyond the arch, a waterwheel can be seen on the opposite side of Stockghyll. At the road turn right, then cross the road to the left and on to follow a short street between Barclays Bank and The Market Hall.

◆ Go left up Stockghyll Lane, between tall trees and with the deep Stockghyll

to the left. In a little way the road levels (with the Howes houses to the right) and an entrance, gap and gate, leads into the woods. Keep along the path, rising to the right, with Stockghyll down to the left. A railed viewpoint stands to the left but the best view to the falls lies just above this. Above both, there is a levelled viewpoint and picnic benches (a wheelchair access track with roadside parking comes in at this point).

◆ Ascend until the path moves left to cross a wooden footbridge beyond the top of the falls. Descend by the path. A viewpoint, now rather overgrown, can be accessed some 100m below the bridge. Continue down the path to cross a wooden footbridge. Return to the original path and, in a little way, exit the woods returning to Stockghyll Lane.

WALK 3

FACT SHEET
LENGTH: ¾ km.
TIME: ¾ hour.
DIFFICULTY: Easy with a little a ascent (75m) and descent.
START & FINISH: Ambleside's Rydal Road main car park (376047).
ALTERNATIVE START: Any of the Ambleside car parks.
MAPS: OS L90 or OL7.
HOSTELRIES: Extensive choice around Ambleside.

The Bridge House

Stockghyll   Waterwheel

Stockghyll Force

WALK 4
WANSFELL ABOVE AMBLESIDE

At the head of Windermere Lake, defined by the Kirkstone Road to the west and Troutbeck to the east, gentle Wansfell watches over the little town of Ambleside. This clockwise circuit leads steeply over Wansfell Pike before descending Nanny Lane down The Hundreds to Troutbeck. It then makes return by a low traverse of Robin Lane reaching Skelghyll Wood to pass the famous viewpoint of Jenkin Crag overlooking Windermere Lake.

THE ROUTE

Behind Ambleside's Market Hall, Cheapside rises to Stockghyll Lane. Ascend the surfaced lane (Stockghyll Force thunders unseen in the woods to the left) until, with the old Kelsick Grammar School to the right (on games day - Wednesdays - we climbed this hill twice), the track passes through a gate and becomes unsurfaced. In a little way an iron ladder stile ascends to the right and leads to a path rising to a further ladder stile over a stone wall. The path steepens through the small oaks to climb directly up the flanks of Wansfell Pike. Keep left at the craggy top to

crest the high rock knoll. The view over Windermere Lake and to the high fells all around cannot fail to take your breath away - however many times you may have seen it.

◆ Cross the stile and bear left, descending the worn path over The Hundreds to join the walled Nanny Lane leading to the Troutbeck Road. The way goes right although a short detour to the left leads to The Mortal Man whose sign may bring a smile;

"Oh mortal man that lives by bread,
What is it makes thy nose so red?
Thou silly fool that looks so pale,
'Tis drinking Sally Birketts ale."

◆ Back on route, a number of wells issue above the road, including Margarets,

START HERE

Stockghyll Force

Stockghyll Lane

AMBLESIDE

Waterhead

Wansfell Pike 1518'

gate

The Hundreds

Nanny

Lane

N

Windermere

Skelghyll Wood

High Skelghyll Farm

Jenkin Crag

cattlegrid

ruin

Hundreds

Road

Troutbeck

Post Office

Low Skelghyll

Robin

Lane

Hol

Beck

1/2 mile

Wansfell above Ambleside

James and St John's, before the post office building stands to the right. Bear right up the track of Robin Lane. The last stone cottage is inscribed 'BB 1732'. Continue to follow the lane until it begins to rise. Here the way leads off to the left (signed Ambleside).

◆ The path/track leads over little Hol Beck before rising briefly to pass High Skelghyll and on to enter Skelghyll Wood. A gap in the wall (and sign) lead to Jenkin Crag. This once popular Victorian view point offers an astonishing view out over Windermere Lake even though the trees now partly obscure the vista. Return to the track which descends gradually to Ambleside to join Lake Road opposite Hayes Garden Centre. Go right back into Ambleside.

FACT SHEET
LENGTH: *10 km.*
TIME: *3½ hours.*
DIFFICULTY: *Difficult with strenuous ascent (450m) though easier descent.*
START & FINISH: *Ambleside's Rydal Road main car park (376047).*
ALTERNATIVE START: *Any of the Ambleside car parks.*
MAPS: *OS L90 or OL7.*
HOSTELRIES: *Enroute are the Mortal Man Inn and Post Office Teas in Troutbeck.*

Windermere Lake from Jenkin Crag

WALK 5
LOUGHRIGG FROM AMBLESIDE

This is the classic outing - rising from Ambleside's Miller Bridge by Todd Crags and Lily Tarn to follow along the shoulder of the fell to the summit which overlooks both Langdale and Grasmere. Descending the northern nose, above Grasmere, leads to Loughrigg Terrace. Return is made by the side of Rydal Water to Rydal's Pelter Bridge and then along the Under Loughrigg Road back to Ambleside.

THE ROUTE

Loughrigg is the low fell which stands above the vales of Ambleside, Rydal and Grasmere. Take the footbridge from the car cark and go right to pass the Bridge House. Bear right along Compston Road and continue until, at the next junction (cinema on corner), Vicarage Road joins the side road and leads to Rothay Park. Follow the main path through the park to emerge by a flat bridge over Stockghyll Beck which leads to the stone arched Miller Bridge over the River Rothay.

◆ Cross Miller Bridge and bear right along the road over the cattle grid until, in a few metres, a steep surfaced road rises to the left. Climb the track to pass the buildings of Brow Head. At the S-bend beyond, a stone stile leads up and off left. The path crosses a narrow footbridge before rising up the open hillside above. A variety of routes are possible, though for the best views over Windermere Lake it is best to keep left before rising to the first rocky knoll. A higher knoll, Todd Crags, follows with definitive views of The Fairfield Horseshoe to the north and Windermere Lake to the south.

◆ Beyond this the way drops right to a well defined path. Follow the path to pass a little pond before cresting a rise and dropping to the lovely little pocket handerchief of Lily Tarn. The path skirts the right edge of the tarn to roughly follow the broad crest of Loughrigg Fell. A gate/stile leads to the base of a further knoll. Ascend and descend the knoll to find a raised track below.

◆ Go left along the main track to cross a little stream, which drains Black Mire then take the path leading

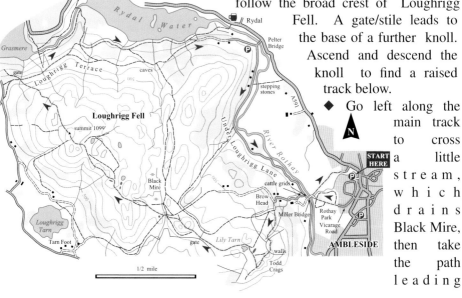

WALK 5

Little Tarn on Loughrigg

right. Follow the path to make steep ascent of the fellside and continue traversing to follow the path down into a hollow. A small tarn to the right. Cross the hollow and keep to the main path which, in a further 450m, gains a narrow corridor. Climb the steps and continue to climb again to the Trig Point on the rocky knoll – the summit of Loughrigg Fell.

◆ Descend the main path in the direction of Grasmere. Stone steps and pitching in places. Near the base of the nose intercept a level track – Loughrigg Terrace. Go right descending to a stone wall by a wood. Proceed along the wall and by the low track which traverses by the shore of Rydal Water. Climb to the main track which leads through the woods above Cote How. At the bottom of the lane turn right and follow the Under Loughrigg Road (for 2km) back to Miller Bridge. Cross the bridge to

Down to Grasmere Lake

bear left to follow the track by the side of Stockghyll Beck. Turn right by the main Rydal Road to find the car park just beyond the Fire Station.

FACT SHEET
LENGTH: *10½ km.*
TIME: *3½ hours.*
DIFFICULTY: *Mildly difficult with straightforward ascent (500m) and descent.*
START & FINISH: *Ambleside's Rydal Road main car park (376047).*
ALTERNATIVE START: *Car park above Pelter Bridge (365060).*
MAPS: *OS L90 or OL7.*
HOSTELRIES: *The Badger Bar in Rydal lies nearby.*

WALK 6
RED SCREES FROM KIRKSTONE

Running above the Kirkstone Road, Red Screes is the name given to the long shoulder rising from Ambleside. The summit and its distinctive cove of red screes stands just to the east of the Kirkstone Pass. To reach the top, altitude 776m, only involves 323m of ascent from the Kirkstone Pass Inn - highest Inn in the Lake District. On the summit will be found a mountain tarn and magnificent views.

THE ROUTE

For experienced fell walkers this may seem a straightforward outing - nevertheless it shouldn't be underestimated for this is a high fell and the weather can deteriorate quickly. In winter, snow and ice are common; the going is strenuous with little respite and it is important to stay on the path as craggy steeps lie to either side.

◆ Exposed in places, the route follows a zigzagging well defined path up the steep fellside to the right of the cove. Quit the car park by the little gate and follow the path leftwards across the boggy hollow. Rise through the flat topped rocky knolls then traverse left before climbing to a little shoulder. Continue above the cove, until the path traverses rightwards. In only a short way, waymarker, the path moves back left, crossing a rock slab to regain the edge of the cove. Continue steeply until the path moves right and the angle eases. Follow the path trending rightwards and rise to the summit - marked by a circular stone shelter and rocky knoll with the Trig Point located just beyond. A small tarn lies just to the south of the summit, fine views extend in all directions.

◆ In descent, reverse the route taken in ascent keeping to the path. (Kilnshaw Chimney marked on the OS map is not a path).

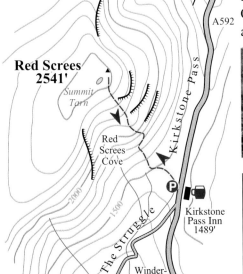

FACT SHEET
LENGTH: *2¼ km.*
TIME: *1¾ hours.*
DIFFICULTY: *Difficult with strenuous ascent (330m) and descent.*
START & FINISH: *Car park opposite the Kirkstone Pass Inn (401081).*
MAPS: *OS L90 or OL7.*
HOSTELRIES: *The Kirkstone Pass Inn.*

WALK 6

Looking up Kirkstone Pass with Red Screes to the left and Kirkstone Pass Inn right

Opposite: The Kirkstone Pass Inn

Over Red Screes summit tarn to Trig Point and summit shelter

IRONMONGERY AND DOMESTIC HARDWARE

Key Cutting - Paint Mixing
Electrical Goods

COMPSTON ROAD
AMBLESIDE, CUMBRIA
LA22 9DR

TEL: (015394) 32138
WWW.JFMARTIN.CO.UK

FRED

F

BOOKS

FRED HOLDSWORTH BOOKSHOP

Central Buildings, Ambleside
Cumbria LA22 9BS

Tel: 015394 33388

www.fredontheweb.co.uk

MAIL ORDER

bilbo's cafe

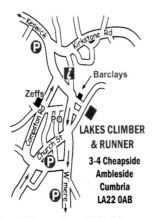

LAKES CLIMBER
& RUNNER

3-4 Cheapside
Ambleside
Cumbria
LA22 0AB

Refueling for Walkers at Lakes Climber & Runner

the ambleside climbing wall

Brand New for 2011.
First class indoor
climbing facility,
with courses for all
abilities, in a fun
and welcoming
environment.

9am—10pm
364 Days a Year
www.adventurepeaks.com
Tel: 015394 33794

STICKLEBARN

TAVERN

Great Langdale, Ambleside, LA22 9JU

Free House

Local Real Ales

Good Homecooked Food

Dogs Welcome

telephone 015394 37356

WALK 7
AMBLESIDE'S HIGH TO LOW SWEDEN BRIDGE

The high valley of Scandale, located on the opposite side of the Red Screes shoulder to Kirksone Pass, drops directly to Ambleside. Tumbling steeply through wooded gorge and over rocky fall, Scandale Beck is crossed by two stone arch bridges. This easy going circuit crosses the two Sweden Bridges by first rising between stone walls and enclosing woods before making descent with an open aspect over lake and fell.

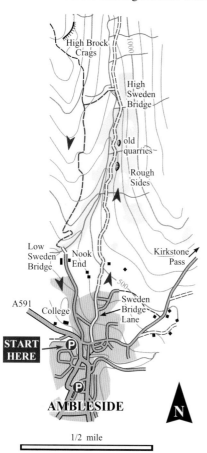

rough stone and occasional cobbling up the old packhorse lane which leads to Scandale Pass. As the track falls slightly to overlook the gorge of Scandale Beck a gate leads into the mixed birch, hazel, oak and ash of Rough Sides Wood.

◆ The track continues to rise past old slate quarries until a lesser track cuts off left. Take this and cross the beck by the ancient flattened stone arch of High Sweden Bridge. Note the name Sweden which comes from the Viking 'Svioinn' meaning 'moorland cleared by burning'.

◆ Rise with the path to intercept a better defined track leading back left down the hillside through the gap in the stone wall marked by a ladder stile.

◆ The open track offers breathtaking views over Loughrigg to the Coniston and Langdale fells and over Rydal Water and Windermere Lake. It leads down to Low Sweden Bridge.

◆ Cross to gain the end of Nook Lane by Nook End Farm. The lane leads back to the Kirkstone Pass road just below the Golden Rule Inn.

THE ROUTE
Opposite the car park the Kirkstone Pass road rises steeply out of Ambleside. Follow this until, some 100 metres past the Golden Rule, Sweden Bridge lane cuts off left. Rise with the lane without deviation, don't turn left, until the surfacing ends at a wooden gate. Continue between stone walls over

WALK 7

High Sweden Bridge

The view over Ambleside to
Windermere Lake

Nook Lane

FACT SHEET
LENGTH: *5 km.*
TIME: *1¾ hours.*
DIFFICULTY: *Easy with gradual ascent (180m) and descent.*
START & FINISH: *Ambleside's Rydal Road main car park (376047).*
MAPS: *OS L90 or OL7.*
HOSTELRIES: *Plentiful in Ambleside, The Golden Rule Inn enroute.*

THE FAIRFIELD HORSESHOE

A classic high fell outing and one of the great mountain walks of the Lake district. Topped by Fairfield, high above the hamlet of Rydal, a rising horseshoe of fells makes a semi circle around the hanging valley of Rydal. The eastern leg of the horseshoe rises from Ambleside and the western leg falls in a long shoulder above Grasmere down to Rydal. The going is straightforward though subject to all the challenges of a high mountain outing.

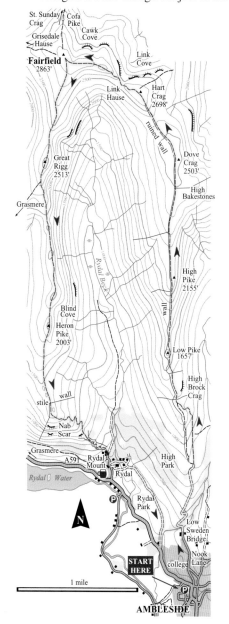

THE ROUTE

This much celebrated round well deserves its popularity. It offers wonderful views over scenes of great beauty and the walking quality is first class throughout. In less than perfect visibility the summit plateau of Fairfield can be misleading.

◆ Cross the road to ascend the Kirkstone Road for a short distance until Nook Lane bears off to the left (the Golden Rule Inn lies just above). Follow the lane which ends at Nook Farm. The track continues across Low Sweden Bridge before rising through the fields. The path is obvious as it rises up the eastern leg of this great horseshoe.

◆ Above the fields, whilst the main path bears right, an alternative follows the crest by the wall, rejoining the main trod a little further on by the craggy little scar of High Brock Crag. Thereafter the path follows the stone wall. Surmounting the craggy face of Low Pike directly involves a short rocky scramble which can be easily bypassed to the right. Rocky Low Pike has a cairned top and already offers a worthwhile view.

◆ Beyond, the path goes left, taking a stile over the wall, then climbs to the gentler height of High Pike. The summit of Dove Crag follows. Descent and slight ascent lead to the stony ridged top of Hart Crag. A cairn marks the highest point. A steep dip into Link Hause is

WALK 8

To Hart Crag and Fairfield

Fairfield Horseshoe above Ambleside

followed by a very stony ascent before the angle eases and the path leads rapidly, up and onto, the great domed summit plateau of Fairfield. The central circular shelter cairn is probably the best stop for this walk.

◆ Before descending the western leg take great care to ensure the correct route is selected. Head initially east, then go south to find the plunge down the shoulder. Make a dip over Calf Cove and ascend to the cairned top of Great Rigg (sometimes called Greatrigg Man). In front lies a scene of matchless beauty. Plunge onward over the undulations of Rydal Fell to its final and definite summit and then on to Heron Pike.

◆ Nab Scar, a prominent cairn and little top, follows. With steep craggy ground, and Rydal Water directly below, bear left following the path down until it intercepts the track which rises from the hamlet of Rydal. Descend the surfaced road, passing Rydal Mount, the final home of William Wordsworth, seen to the right. A track bears off to the left. This passes above Rydal Hall before making a lovely return through Rydal Park to the A591 just outside of Ambleside.

FACT SHEET
LENGTH: *17 km.*
TIME: *7 hours.*
DIFFICULTY: *A difficult and long mountain route with sustained ascent (875m) and descent.*
START & FINISH: *Ambleside's Rydal Road main car park (376047).*
MAPS: *OS L90 or OL7.*
HOSTELRIES: *Plentiful in Ambleside, The Golden Rule Inn enroute.*

WALK 9
AROUND THE VALE OF RYDAL

A pleasant stroll on which to experience the ambiance of this delightful area around the hamlet of Rydal. With strong Wordsworth connections it follows a clockwise circuit to explore Dora's Field and Rydal Church before passing by Rydal Hall and through Rydal Park. Return is made from Scandale Bridge taking Rydal Steps beneath Field Foot to pass Pelter Bridge.

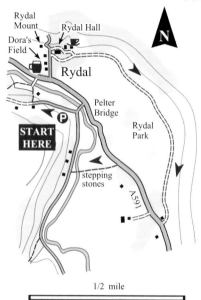

1/2 mile

FACT SHEET
LENGTH: *4 km.*
TIME: *1 hour.*
DIFFICULTY: *Easy.*
START & FINISH: *Pelter Bridge car park (364060).*
MAPS: *OS L90 or OL7.*
HOSTELRIES: *The Badger Bar and The Old School Room Tea Shop (Rydal Hall) are all enroute.*

THE ROUTE

Rydal Mount was the home of William Wordsworth between 1813 and 1850. This walk passes just below the house after making an exploration of Dora's Field, named after Wordsworth's favourite daughter, noted for its wonderful display of golden daffodils.

◆ From the car park, go left to climb the road until, opposite Cote How Cottages, a kissing gate on the right leads to steps down through Steps End Wood. Beyond the wood the path leads down rightwards over the field to the footbridge crossing the River Rothay. Rise to the A591 and with the Badger Bar opposite, cross the road with care. Go right, along the footpath, for only

a little way until a signed iron gate on the left opens into Dora's Field. Enter and make a clockwise circuit of the 'field', first ascending to the left before descending to leave by the iron kissing gate entering the grounds of Rydal Church. There is open access to this fine little church (a donation to Church Funds is always greatly appreciated). Walk through the church garden to gain the lane.

◆ Exit left onto the road (Rydal Mount lies a little higher) and then take the lane to the right to pass behind the back of Rydal Hall. The track leads between the buildings associated with the hall, over a bridge and on rightwards, through the rhododendrons and exotic trees of Rydal Park. Continue along the lane. In season Rydal Sheep Dog Trials and Ambleside Show, are held in the fields to the right. Exit through great iron gates onto the A591 by Scandale Bridge.

◆ Cross the road and go right, on the pavement, to follow by the invariably

Rydal Hall

Daffodils, Dora's Field

time of writing) - take a line bearing diagonally right to a levelling in the shoulder of the hill opposite. Continue, passing to the right of a cluster of oaks, to intercept the stepping stones of Rydal Steps situated at the far corner of the field. Cross the River Rothay, impossible in times of heavy rain, and go right along the road to bear left by Pelter Bridge back to the car park.

Rydal Steps

busy A591 for 500 metres until a kissing gate (signed) gives access to the field on the left just beyond a tree clad knoll (beyond the cricket field). There is no obvious path across the field (at the

WALK 10
THE ROUND OF RYDAL WATER

Nestling amidst an area of exquisite beauty, one known and celebrated worldwide for its association with William Wordsworth and the Lake Poets, this walk makes a reasonably gentle anticlockwise perambulation of Rydal Water. With a fine aspect over Rydal it first rises to Loughrigg Terrace before traversing to Rydal Caves. It then drops to Rydal village to rise once again to follow the Coffin Road. Finally it crosses White Moss Common Fell with a magnificent view to both Rydal Water and Grasmere lake.

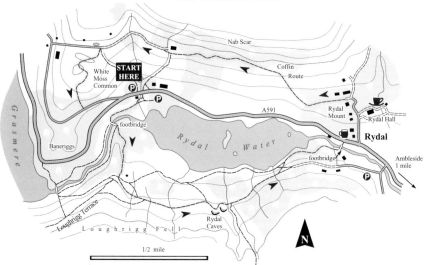

THE ROUTE

From either car park walk towards the River Rothay. Cross the wooden footbridge and continue straight on, following the path that leads through the woods, away from the river. A kissing gate emerges from the woods onto a stony track.

◆ Take the path above, ascending the hillside through the bracken to gain a level path known as Loughrigg Terrace. Traverse left along the terrace path until the entrance to Rydal Cave is encountered - old slate quarry.

◆ Descend the stony track, through the larch, below the quarry and pass a further quarry until the track descends to the path above the shore of Rydal

---

FACT SHEET
LENGTH: *6 km.*
TIME: *2¾ hours.*
DIFFICULTY: *Easy with slight ascent (140m) and descent.*
START & FINISH: White Moss Common car parks (348066).
MAPS: *OS L90 or OL7.*
HOSTELRIES: *Joseph's Ice Cream Van at White Moss Common. The Badger Bar and The Old School Room Tea Shop (Rydal Hall) all in Rydal at the half way point. The Badger Bar and The Old School Room Tea Shop (Rydal Hall) are enroute.*

Water. Go down right to, just above the water's edge, enter the oak woods through a little iron gate. Beyond the wood cross the field and drop left to cross the river, flowing from the lake, by a narrow wooden footbridge.

◆ Bear right along the road until in 100m the lane on the left is ascended. This passes Rydal Mount, the final home of William Wordsworth, to find a track traversing left above the house. This is the old Coffin Road between Ambleside and Grasmere.

◆ Stony in places, the track is well defined, traversing through clumps of oaks with a view south over Rydal Water. As the track rounds a bend and intercepts a wall there is a rectangular flat topped stone on the right. This is the coffin rest stone. There is a seat beyond this. A little further along the track a gate leads through a wall to enter woods (high above Nab Cottage).

◆ Keep along the track and pass through a gate, to dip slightly, before making a short steep ascent. Round the shoulder and make a stepped rocky descent to cross a stream and join a larger unsurfaced track – which serves the house just above to the right. Keep on the level track. Cross over a brow where the road becomes surfaced, passing a house up to the right, and descend until a track falls down steeply to the left and a pond stands to the right.

◆ Don't take the track but cross a little wooden footbridge, opposite the end of the pond, to the left. Climb the fellside and round the first rock hillock to the left. On the shoulder there is a small bench and an open view over Rydal

Rydal Water

Water. Continue along the path to gain a little brackened corridor between the hummocks. Bear right to cross the head of a boggy area until in a little way, the craggy end of another, the highest, largest hummock stands to the left. Pick the easiest way through the rock slabs and ascend to the summit plateau. This is the top of White Moss Common Fell - a superb viewpoint looking out over both the vale of Rydal and the vale of Grasmere.

◆ Walk to the end and take the path, descending left, towards Rydal Water. After a short section of descent the path veers right a little to pass by an old pond, masked by trees, ringed by an ancient iron fence. Continue down the shoulder, the path is narrow and there are a few little rocky steps, until the way leads over to the surfaced road. Bear left down the road to the car parks.

Rydal Cave

WALK 11
WHITE MOSS COMMON TO GRASMERE LAKE BY THE RIVER ROTHAY

Short and simple, this is a walk of contrast and quality. It crosses the River Rothay by two wooden footbridges making an anticlockwise, although easily reversible, circuit through Baneriggs Wood to visit the foot of Grasmere Lake before returning along the river by Loughrigg Wood. In May the woods are carpeted with bluebells though this is very much a walk for all seasons and most weather conditions.

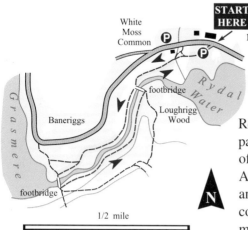

magnificent oaks. Slight descent leads to a footbridge and a crossing made of the River Rothay.

♦ A short walk right leads to the base of Grasmere lake and a fine view. Return along the well constructed path/track following the south bank of the river to enter Loughrigg Wood. A remarkable stand of silver birch and a sea of bluebells in early May, coupled with birdsong and the happy murmurings of the river make this an enchanting place. Continue along the track, which rises slightly with an unfenced drop to the river, before the path drops to the footbridge to lead back to White Moss Common.

THE ROUTE

Often it's the simplest things in life that provide the most pleasure; a single snowflake drifting from a wintry sky, a ray of sunshine piercing grey cloud. So it is with this short, lovely walk to Grasmere lake. Beginning from the lower car park avoids having to make a crossing of the road. Leave the back of the car park to follow the track, over a small footbridge, to the bend in the river. A favourite swimming/paddling area in summer, much frequented by swans and ducks looking for titbits. Continue to the wooden footbridge, supported on stone pillars, which crosses the River Rothay.

♦ Don't cross the bridge, but take the gate on its right and follow the track along the field edge. Gain Baneriggs Woods and rise through the

Swans by White Moss Common

WALK 11

Looking over Grasmere Lake and Rydal Water

White Moss Common

Bluebells in May

FACT SHEET
LENGTH: *2½ km.*
TIME: *1 hour.*
DIFFICULTY: *Easy.*
START & FINISH: *White Moss Common car parks (348066).*
MAPS: *OS L90 or OL7.*
HOSTELRIES: *Joseph's Ice Cream Van by higher car park.*

WALK 12
TO ALCOCK TARN ABOVE GRASMERE

Alcock Tarn nestles high above Grasmere, hidden behind Butter Crags within a fold of Heron Pike. Offering unrivalled views over the Vale of Grasmere, this route passes by Dove Cottage and Town End duck pond to ascend through the trees of Wood Close and then the open fell, before rounding Butter Crags to overlook little Alcock Tarn. A descent of the zigzags leads to Greenhead Gill before a footpath across the fields leads directly back to the car park.

THE ROUTE

Head out of the village to cross the main road. Bear left through Town End to pass by Wordsworth's famous former home, Dove Cottage. Continue up the lane to pass a duck pond (badly overgrown) opposite How Top Farm. Bear left at the junction and climb the steep hill until, in a further 180 metres an unsurfaced track (signed Alcock Tarn) bears off to the left.

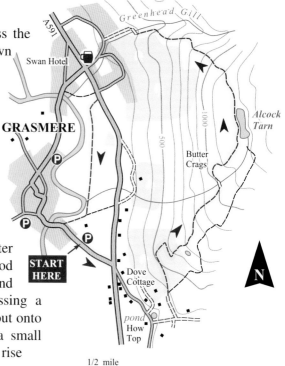

◆ Rise to a gate and take it to enter the mixed beech woods of Wood Close. Keep along the track and rise to a junction. Bear right, passing a little man made pond, to move out onto open fell. Continue through a small iron gate in the stone wall and rise again to cross the little beck over a tiny stone arch bridge - the smallest in Lakeland. Contour beneath the rocky knoll of Butter Crags (labelled Grey Crag by the OS) and ascend to the grassy shoulder. Breathtaking views extend over the vale of Grasmere. Cross through a gap in the stone wall to overlook Alcock Tarn. A further gap in the wall leads out left to provide a breathtaking view.

◆ Traverse by the tarn to gain and follow the path which leads down to make steep descent of the zigzags. Keeping above the forestry wall, descend to the edge of Greenhead Gill and follow down this until it can be crossed by a little wooden footbridge.

◆ A surfaced track leads through trees and past houses to emerge into the open by a quiet road. Bear first left then right to arrive at the Swan Inn by the side of the main A591. Go left to find a crossing point and cross the road.

WALK 12

Looking over Alcock Tarn

View to Helm Crag

Dove Cottage

Go left until the second signed footpath heads right across the fields. The path is well signed, though muddy in wet weather, and leads first to the banks of the River Rothay, then passes converted cottages, once 'THE WORKMAN'S READING ROOM', to finally pass by Grasmere School and on to Stock Lane.

FACT SHEET
LENGTH: *5 km.*
TIME: *2 hours.*
DIFFICULTY: *Mildly difficult with ascent (320m) and descent.*
START & FINISH: *Grasmere, Stock Lane Car Park (339072).*
MAPS: *OS L90 or OL7.*
HOSTELRIES: *Plentiful in Grasmere, the Swan Inn passed enroute.*

WALK 13
GRASMERE VILLAGE WALK

A delightful clockwise perambulation which savours much of the ambiance of this attractive archetypal Lakeland village. Footbridges across the River Rothay lead to the Church and Gingerbread House. Sam Read's Bookshop and Heaton Cooper's Studio are passed to gain the road rising to Wordsworth's former home, Allan Bank. Descent to the Easedale Road and a rounding of Butterlip How continues to White Bridge before a traverse of the park heads back to the car park and ancient rock carvings.

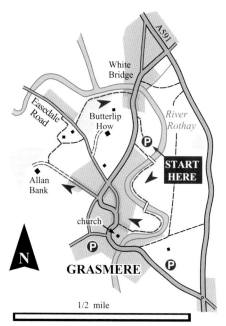

THE ROUTE

From the back of the car park, cross the footbridge and bear right, along the delightful tree lined footpath beside the clear waters of the River Rothay. Round the bend in the river, pass the private bridge leading into the village, and continue to a further wooden footbridge. Bear left and continue along the path, pass by another footbridge which leads to a path by the school, and continue to wind a way, beside the church standing to the left, to an exit through the stone wall onto the pavement beside the Gingerbread House. An arch on the right provides entrance to St Oswalds churchyard and the graves of William Wordsworth and family.

◆ Bear right, and follow College St. until, at Sam Read's Bookshop take a turn left along the road. Pass the Heaton Cooper Studio to find a little surfaced road leading up to the right. Continue up the road to leave the village and climb until a large house, William Wordsworth's former home, Allan Bank, stands on its own amongst the trees up to the left. Just beyond, a waymarked grassy track drops down to the right towards a large white building. At the building a Permissive Path goes left around the building and through a kissing gate to follow along the edge of the field.

FACT SHEET
LENGTH: *2½ km.*
TIME: *¾ hour.*
DIFFICULTY: *Easy, with slight ascent (30m) and descent.*
START & FINISH: *Grasmere village central car park (339078).*
MAPS: *OS L90 or OL7.*
HOSTELRIES: *Plentiful in Grasmere.*

Grasmere Church

Beside the River Rothay

◆ In 130m the Easedale Road lies on the other side of the hedge and a little further an opening leads onto the road. Go right, down the road, until by the end of the cottages on the left there is a wooden gate. Turn left through the gate and follow the path through the trees of Butterlip How (spelt Butharlyp Howe on OS) with the River Rothay down below to the left. Emerge onto the main Grasmere Road by White Bridge and cross the road. Go right, passing Rothay Garden Hotel, until entrance can be made into the park. Follow the path along the edge of the park back to the car park. Carved in the top of the rocky knoll, reached by scrambling, find prehistoric cup markings.

Sam Read's Bookshop in centre of village

badger press

Environmental Award Winning Design & Print in Lakeland

We are very pleased to be associated with Bill Birkett and share his love of the Lakes and concern for the environment.

Check out our website for information of all our services:

www.badgerpress.co.uk

LANGDALE CO-OP
VILLAGE STORE

Set on two floors in the picturesque village of Chapel Stile, we provide the complete shopping experience. Downstairs is a traditional grocery store, stocking all types of food, plus a large selection of beers and wines. Upstairs is a versatile Alladin's Cave of gifts, toys, outdoors gear, hardware and lots more. Friendly and attentive staff.

Opening Times:
Daily: 9am – 5.30pm

Tel: 015394 37260

SamRead
Bookseller
Grasmere

Established 1887

Walking Books, Maps, Guides
Classics and Poetry
Popular Science
and Philosophy
Arts and Crafts
Children's Books

...and much more

Book search and ordering service

Telephone: 015394 35374

email:
books@samread.co.uk

www.samreadbooks.co.uk

www.threeshiresinn.co.uk

Local real ales, home cooked food, wonderful views, cosy bedrooms await you when you visit the Three Shires Inn......
Welcome to the unspoilt valley of Little Langdale

Three Shires Inn, Little Langdale, LA22 9NZ
015394 37215   enquiry@threeshiresinn.co.uk

Bill Birkett
Photo Courses

Learn about landscape & mountain photography whilst walking the fells and dales with Bill Birkett.

Courses can be suited to individual requirements.

Individual & small groups catered for.

Daily rates available.

Tel: 015394 37329
email: bill.birkett1@btopenworld.com
www.billbirkett.co.uk

WEARINGS
BOOKSHOP

Ordnance Survey Maps
Lakeland Walking Guides
A.Wainwright Books
& Signed Prints

Beatrix Potter Tales
& Children Books

Lake Road, Ambleside 015394 32312

OPEN 7 DAYS A WEEK

WALK 14
ALONG HUNTINGSTILE AND DOW BANK FROM HIGH CLOSE

This pleasant round combines open fellside and slopes of mixed woodland in a delightful position with views over both Grasmere and Great Langdale. From the high point of the Grasmere to Elterwater road the route strikes west along the Huntingstile shoulder to ascend, or traverse by, the conical top of Dow Bank. Descent from here towards Grasmere by Wyke Wood, is followed by an ascent of the Huntingstile track.

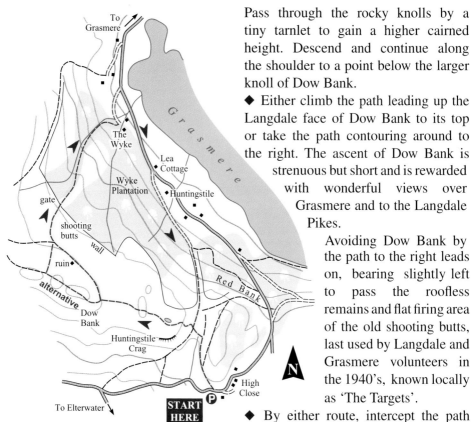

Pass through the rocky knolls by a tiny tarnlet to gain a higher cairned height. Descend and continue along the shoulder to a point below the larger knoll of Dow Bank.

◆ Either climb the path leading up the Langdale face of Dow Bank to its top or take the path contouring around to the right. The ascent of Dow Bank is strenuous but short and is rewarded with wonderful views over Grasmere and to the Langdale Pikes.

Avoiding Dow Bank by the path to the right leads on, bearing slightly left to pass the roofless remains and flat firing area of the old shooting butts, last used by Langdale and Grasmere volunteers in the 1940's, known locally as 'The Targets'.

◆ By either route, intercept the path which crosses the shoulder between Dow Bank and Spedding Crag to bear right and make descent. The path passes through the juniper, by two level shooting areas, to find a gate in the wall on the edge of Wyke Plantation. A path leads down through mixed woods to swing left and follow above the stream with a wall to the right. An old iron kissing gate leads onto a surfaced driveway.

THE ROUTE

Above the road, on the Langdale side of the cattle grid, ascend the grassy path around onto the open fellside. The route crosses the deep dip, a natural little valley rift which crosses over the shoulder of the fell, then climbs steeply up the end of Huntingstile Crag.

Looking to Dow Bank with Great Langdale seen beyond

The Huntingstile gate with Grasmere below

◆ Bear left down the driveway to the road. Swing right and follow the road for 400 metres until, opposite a red post box in the wall of Lea Cottage, a surfaced lane ascends to the right.

◆ Follow the lane, pass Hunting Stile Lodge, to continue along the ascending stony track. At its head, by a metal bench and resting place, the middle high gate leads to open ground. Continue by the wall, with Redbank Wood to the left, to follow above the little valley which cuts down from the heights. Continue on to a gate in the wall to regain the boggy dip in the shoulder just below the point at which the original path climbs Huntingstile Crag.

FACT SHEET
LENGTH: *4¼ km.*
TIME: *2 hours.*
DIFFICULTY: *Mildly difficult with moderate ascent (300m) and descent.*
START & FINISH: *High Close, beyond the cattle grid there are limited roadside parking spaces on the Langdale side (338052).*
MAPS: *OS L90 or OL7.*
HOSTELRIES: *Non enroute.*

WALK 15
TO BLIND TARN AND SILVER HOW

Silver How is the dominant little fell standing to the west of Grasmere lake and is a favourite viewpoint. It offers a lovely aspect over the vales of both Grasmere and Rydal. This walk, approaching by Lower Easedale and the secretive Blind Tarn basin, now a moss, provides a fascinating contrast with the openness of the tops, before delightful descent leads through juniper and bracken directly back to Allan Bank and Grasmere.

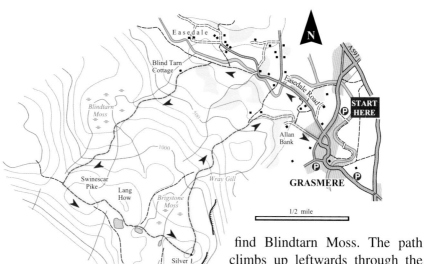

THE ROUTE

Gain and follow the delightful Easedale Road rising directly from the centre of Grasmere. In some 900m the road levels and rounds a right bend to reveal, on the left, a small footbridge crossing Easedale Beck. Cross and follow the path through the little wood and on through the fields until a gated track leads off to the left.

◆ Follow the track to the converted farm buildings and pass through the gate beyond onto the rough fellside. A vague, wet, path leads steeply up by the wall then straight up the fellside to a higher wall. The path/track goes right beneath the wall and rises above Blindtarn Gill to gain the lip of the basin. In the hollow, the flat area which was once Blind Tarn,

find Blindtarn Moss. The path climbs up leftwards through the juniper, all the time aiming for the lowest point on the skyline – the distinct col of Swinescar Hause.

◆ On gaining the grassy col, the going eases and the path leads to the right of the knoll of Swinescar Pike. On the Langdale side of the knoll, bear left following the main path up the broad shoulder. Stay with the path, which falls slightly to pass Lang How, the distinct knoll to the left, and Youdell Tarn, now heavily choked with reeds, to the right. Pass a further two lesser tarns then take the narrow path leading off to the right.

◆ Traverse the path, cross a boggy hollow, then climb to the cairned top of Silver How and stunning views over Grasmere. Immediately to the north of the top, follow the path which falls steeply, before levelling and continuing

WALK 15

to make a rocky descent and crossing of the little ravine of Wray Gill. Beyond the Gill, bear right and continue along until the path swings left to make descent through the stand of ancient juniper.

◆ With open views over the vale of Grasmere make steep descent by a stone wall before traversing left to regain and continue by the wall. The path swings left to a kissing gate leading to a narrow track between the walls. Descend the track keeping right of the cottages to gain a surfaced lane. Bear right and continue down the track, which passes the large house of Allan Bank standing to the right, and down to the main road through Grasmere. Head left back to the car park.

FACT SHEET
LENGTH: *8 km.*
TIME: *3¼ hours.*
DIFFICULTY: *Difficult with steep ascent (425m) and descent.*
START & FINISH: *Grasmere village central car park (339078).*
MAPS: *OS L90 or OL7.*
HOSTELRIES: *Plentiful in Grasmere, non enroute.*

Above Blindtarn Moss

Silver How above Grasmere Lake

WALK 16
A CIRCUIT OF EASEDALE TARN

In many respects this is the definitive 'Grasmere' walk, rising from the village to explore the secrets and immense beauty of high Easdale, its hidden tarn and tumbling waterfalls. Beyond the meadows and stone buildings of Easedale this route enters Far Easedale to cross the beck at Stythwaite Steps to make a rising traverse to the tarn. A rounding of the tarn is followed by descent alongside the waterfalls of Sourmilk Gill to pass Brimmer Head Farm and return to the Easedale Road.

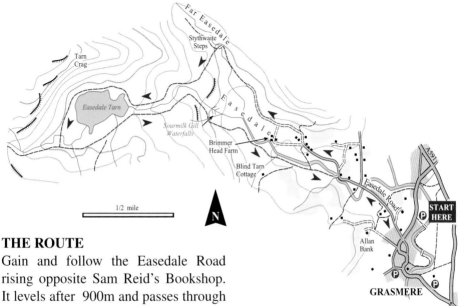

THE ROUTE

Gain and follow the Easedale Road rising opposite Sam Reid's Bookshop. It levels after 900m and passes through an iron gate to continue through the meadows. Walk by the buildings and bear right ascending a stony track. Go through the gate and walled opening, amidst the trees, to exit by making descent down the lane to the left.

◆ Follow the stony lane for 1¼km until the going levels beside Far Easedale Gill and a footbridge and stepping stones – Stythwaite Steps – make a crossing. Beyond the bridge make ascent of the well defined path and continue traversing, by stepping stones across the boggy sections, finally rising to the foot of idyllic Easedale Tarn. It is possible to cross the stepping stones beneath the tarn and join the regular path above. However, to get a real taste of this special mountain environment, make an anticlockwise circuit around the tarn. Go right and follow the path, which is well defined, until at the head of the tarn it is best to keep on the high ground to the right to avoid the worst of the boggy sections. Bear left, through an opening in the bracken, to make a crossing of the narrow stream before rising to the main path. Go left down the path back to the foot of the tarn. Note the large boulder beside the path which was once the site of a teahouse.

WALK 16

Idyllic Easedale Tarn

Sourmilk Gill

Site of the old teahouse by Easedale Tarn

◆ Descend the main path to the right of the gill eventually passing the delightful tumbling waterfalls of Sourmilk Gill. The path levels and, through a kissing gate, becomes a well defined stony track. Follow the track, without deviation, to make a crossing of the little footbridge leading onto the Easedale Road. Bear right and descend to Grasmere.

FACT SHEET
LENGTH: *9½ km.*
TIME: *3¼ hours.*
DIFFICULTY: *Mildly difficult with moderate ascent (350m) and descent.*
START & FINISH: *Grasmere village central car park (339078).*
MAPS: *OS L90 or OL7.*
HOSTELRIES: *Plentiful in Grasmere, non enroute.*

WALK 17
HELM CRAG FROM GRASMERE

Helm Crag, noted for its 'Lion & Lamb' rock formations, is the distinctive cockscomb like fell rising directly behind Grasmere. This clockwise circular walk begins through Easedale to rise by the old slate quarries before swinging first left and then back right to ascend the upper section of the distinctive nose of the fell. A traverse of the upper crest passes two distinctive rock outcrops before descent is made down to the valley of Greenburn.

THE ROUTE

Gain and follow the Easedale Road rising opposite Sam Read's Bookshop. The going levels after 900m and passes through an iron gate to walk through the meadows. Pass between the buildings and bear right, ascending a stony track. Go through the gate and walled opening, amidst the trees, to exit by a walled lane branching right and out onto open fellside by the site of the old slate quarries.

◆ After initial ascent to pass the quarry workings, the path zigs leftwards to

<table>
<tr><td>

FACT SHEET
LENGTH: *6¾ km.*
TIME: *2¾ hours.*
DIFFICULTY: *Difficult with steep ascent (380m) and descent.*
START & FINISH: *Grasmere village central car park (339078).*
MAPS: *OS L90 or OL7.*
HOSTELRIES: *Plentiful in Grasmere, Travellers Rest Inn enroute.*

</td></tr>
</table>

traverse left above Helm Crag (Jackdaw Crag on OS map). It then climbs a little before traversing left again around White Crag, then zagging right and making ascent to the nose of Helm Crag. The vista, across Grasmere Lake and into the hanging valley containing Easedale Tarn, is already extensive. Make the final section of steepish ascent to top the first rocky pinnacle at the south east end of the summit ridge. This is the 'Lion & Lamb' formation of rocks seen from the village.

◆ Traverse along the shoulder to the final high pinnacle on the north west end of the summit crest. This is the highest point of Helm Crag, known as the 'Howitzer' when viewed from here. However, when viewed from the lower part of Dunmail Raise, this pinnacle is also known as the 'Lion & Lamb' and it transforms again, into 'The Old Women Playing The Organ', the higher up the

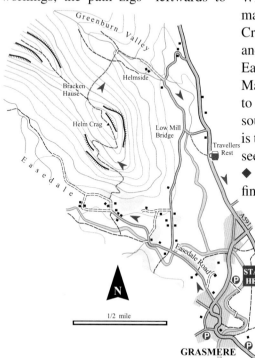

1/2 mile

The summit finger of Helm Crag can only be reached by climbing

Pass you go. Whatever name you give this rocky finger, its top can only be reached by rock climbing.

◆ Continue, to drop to the col of Bracken Hause. Go right from here, down the path, making steep descent first through the bracken then following the steep grassy fellside. Continue beside the stone wall. Pass through a gap in the stone wall which runs across below, and keep down in the same line to cross the abandoned stone walled track through the gaps in the walls (the upper one open and the lower one with kissing gate at the time of writing). Continue down the path through the field below to find a wooden footbridge crossing Greenburn Beck.

◆ Bear right, following the track, rising slightly to a junction of ways just above the walled garden of the large house (unseen) of Helmside. Take the low gate on the left and continue directly down the surfaced lane to the road below. Bear right down the road and turn left to cross Low Mill Bridge. Beyond the bridge a signed footpath leads off to the right. Cross the stepping stones and continue across the field to exit onto the main road opposite the Travellers Rest Inn. Cross and follow the footpath, beside the road, until a little road leads off right to pass the cemetery back into the village.

Helm Crag above Grasmere

WALK 18
STONE ARTHUR ABOVE GRASMERE

Stone Arthur, romantically perpetuating the Arthurian legend, is the striking castle-like rock bastion high above and to the east of Grasmere. The walk described here makes a clockwise arc to top the knoll, rising from Greenhead Gill and falling to Tongue Gill. Exceedingly pleasant in execution, the walk offers wonderful contrasting views and is interesting throughout.

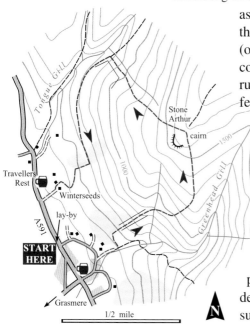

ascends and then bears right between the stone walls of the ancient track (out-gang). Cross the open stream and continue traversing right between the ruinous walls to gain the shoulder of the fell.

◆ Climb the shoulder, which rises from the bracken to become open and grassy, continuing directly to the distinct cairned rocky top of Stone Arthur. The crags below, unprotected drops, offer exceptional views over the vale of Grasmere.

◆ Although there is no definite path the going is easy throughout the descent. Head down west from the summit by a steep grassy slope which leads by an old ruin. Continue down the grass, bearing left to top the rocky knolls. Descend directly down from the knolls, keeping to the right of the stone wall. At the bottom of the stone wall intercept a track. Go left, passing the bottom corner of the wall, and continue along beneath the wall with the old reservoir down below.

◆ Go through the gates and enter a lane, stone paved for a short section, between the stone walls (in-gang). Follow along the lane until, near its end, pass through a kissing gate on the right. Drop steeply down the rough pasture, passing ancient hollow ash, to join a muddy track. Go left and pass through the gate to drop

THE ROUTE

Stone Arthur is actually the truncated terminus of the shoulder which falls towards Grasmere from Great Rigg; the latter is one of the tops found on the western leg of The Fairfield Horseshoe. Follow the lane opposite the lay-by and continue around this lane until a signpost, Greenhead Gill, points left to an ascent up a narrow tree clad track. Continue, with the open stream to the right, to pass through a gate out on to the open fell.

◆ Go left, climbing the steep track which runs by the walled conifer plantation. At the top of the plantation the way first

WALK 18

Making ascent of Stone Arthur

Stone Arhur above Grasmere

Stone Arhur - the top.

down right until, above the buildings, a gate leads right to pass a barn and down through the buildings of Winterseeds. Descend the lane to join the road and, with the Travellers Rest Inn to the right, go left beside the A591 to regain the lay-by.

FACT SHEET
LENGTH: *4¾ km.*
TIME: *2¾ hours.*
DIFFICULTY: *Difficult with steep ascent (440m) and descent.*
START & FINISH: *Lay-by beside the northbound A591 just outside Grasmere (338085).*
MAPS: *OS L90 or OL7.*
HOSTELRIES: *Plentiful in Grasmere, Travellers Rest Inn just off route.*

WALK 19
SEAT SANDAL

Rising from the pass of Dunmail Raise above Grasmere, the curving shoulder of Seat Sandal forms an unmistakeable profile. The route described here offers a straightforward walk to the summit of a high fell. Rising by its South Ridge and falling to Grisedale Hause, before descending by the cascades of Tongue Gill, it provides a splendid outing.

THE ROUTE

Cross the road from the junction by Mill Bridge, watching carefully for traffic in both directions, to follow up the lane by the cottages. Pass the highest house and keep along the stony track.

◆ To make a direct ascent of the south ridge; find, in little way a gate on the left, with a small stone barn below. Go through this gate and immediately turn right up the hill. A track is intercepted and this is followed to rise up to the left and on through a gap in the stone wall. Climb the nose slightly left of the wall and continue to a gate in the next wall. Beyond this, climb the steepening nose to exit by a narrow gate in the fell wall.

◆ Should the gate be locked or a gentler approach preferred; continue up the stony track to cross Little Tongue Gill by a wooden footbridge. Turn left and take the low track on the left, rising beside the gill. Continue by a little path beside the gill until above the stone wall on the left. Traverse left, just above the fell wall, continuing to gain the nose of the south ridge by the little fell wall gate described above.

◆ Climb the undulating nose above by a narrow but well defined path. It levels across the upper crest of the shoulder

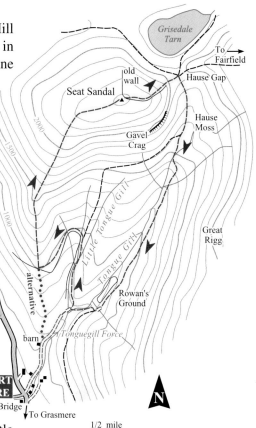

and leads to the summit cairn, reached just before the ruined stone wall. Mighty Fairfield stands above and opposite but this is a high fell sanctuary with outstanding views in all directions.

◆ Continue straight on to take the path descending by the wall to the col of Hause Gap. It steepens nearing the bottom and becomes a little scrambly. Grisedale Tarn lies to the left but go right, through the gap in the low wall, to

Seat Sandal above Grasmere

Looking to Seat Sandal

Down to Hause Gap

follow the path down Hause Moss. Keep left at the fork beneath Gavel Crag. Continue past the tumbling waterfalls to follow on above the true left side of Tongue Gill.

◆ Pass the walled enclosure of Rowan's Ground and continue to descend to a footbridge crossing the gill. Cross the next footbridge over Little Tongue Gill and go left to return to Mill Bridge down the stony track.

FACT SHEET
LENGTH: *7¾ km.*
TIME: *3½ hours.*
DIFFICULTY: *Difficult with steep ascent (700m) and descent.*
START & FINISH: *Wide verge by Mill Bridge junction beside the northbound A591 just outside Grasmere (336092).*
MAPS: *OS L90 or OL7.*
HOSTELRIES: *Plentiful in Grasmere, Travellers Rest Inn nearby.*

WALK 20
RISING FROM DUNMAIL RAISE TO ROUND GRISEDALE TARN

Defeated in battle, King Dunmail is said to be buried beneath the large pile of stones now lying between the split carriageways of the A591 at the head of the eponymous Dunmail Raise Pass. His followers escaped up the path beside Raise Beck and threw his crown into Grisedale Tarn for safe keeping. This is the walk, which also includes The Brothers Parting Stone, so good luck and remember me if you should see that glint of gold.

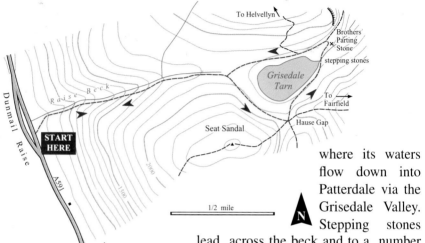

THE ROUTE

Because you start from an altitude of some 235m, this is a good way to minimise the effort in visiting a high mountain tarn in a dramatic setting. Nevertheless the going is rough and it is subject to all the vagaries of mountain weather. Care should also be taken in parking beside and departing onto this busy trunk road.

◆ Cross the stile and follow the path through the bracken to rise steeply up the true left bank (right as you look at it) of Raise Beck. Near the top of the pass, as it levels, the going becomes a little boggy. Head right, around Grisedale Tarn. There is a good stony track which leads first towards Grisedale Hause and then to the foot of the tarn from

where its waters flow down into Patterdale via the Grisedale Valley. Stepping stones lead across the beck and to a number of rocky knolls, looking over the tarn, which provide a good place to picnic on a sunny day.

◆ The Brothers Parting Stone, where William Wordsworth and his brother Jonathan parted in 1805 before the latter was shipwrecked and drowned, will be found a little way down to the left of the stream and is marked by a horizontal metal sign. The inscription faces downstream towards Grisedale. The first line reads *"HERE DID WE STOP; AND HERE LOOKED ROUND"*.

◆ Find the path to the north of the stone and traverse above the shore back to the col at the head of the Raise Beck pass. The path is wet and muddy in places and the higher route is generally the best option. Descend the same path back to the start.

WALK 20

Grisedale Tarn with Fairfield standing beyond

Crossing the foot of
Grisedale Tarn

The Brothers Parting
Stone

FACT SHEET
LENGTH: *6 km.*
TIME: *2½ hours.*
DIFFICULTY: *Difficult with steep rough ascent (425m) and descent.*
START & FINISH: *Wide verge by the stile off the southbound carriage of the A591 atop Dunmail Raise Pass (328116).*
MAPS: *OS L90 or OL7.*
HOSTELRIES: *Non enroute.*

the good life
cottage company

Whether you are looking for a romantic break, family fun or a cosy homecoming, we have a place that's just right for you...

Self Catering Cottages in the English Lake District

Please call Heather or Ben on: **+44 (0) 15394 37417**

Email us at: **stay@thegoodlifecottageco.co.uk**

www. thegoodlifecottageco.co.uk

PET FRIENDLY

★★★ – ★★★★★

THE
BRITANNIA
— INN —

Elterwater
Nr Ambleside
Cumbria LA22 9HP
Tel: 015394 37210
Fax: 015396 78075
email:
info@britinn.co.uk
www.britinn.co.uk

A 500 year old Lakeland inn nestled in the picturesque Langdale Valley. Well appointed double and twin rooms.

Open 7 days a week
from 10.30 am - 11.00 pm

Lunch
12 noon - 2.00 pm

Afternoon Snacks
2.00 pm - 5.30 pm

Evening Meals
6.30 pm - 9.00 pm

Extensive home cooked menu with daily specials to complement our selection of real ales and fine wines. Join us for our weekly quiz night most Sundays of the year.

10% Discount on food and drink upon producing this advert - min £10